LOST

The Truth You Must Know to

IN

Enhance Student Engagement and

SPACE

Increase School Flexibility

Dr. Joseph C. Kosiorek, AIA

Foreword By: Anita Johnson

Copyright © 2021 by ABI Road, LLC

All rights reserved. Except as permitted under the U.S. Copyright Act of 1976, no part of this publication may be reproduced, distributed, or transmitted in any form or by any means, or stored in a database or retrieval system, without the prior written permission of the author, Dr. Joseph C. Kosiorek.

Cover Design: Chris Goldan

Author Photograph: © Gene Avallone

Editor: Maura Grace Harrington Logue, Ph.D.

First Edition: June 2021

ISBN 978-0-578-91230-1

Printed in the United States of America

www.ABIroadLLC.com

To My Family

Acknowledgments

I have so many people to thank. I feel humbled by the opportunity to work with so many brilliant and generous individuals and groups. Without their wisdom and guidance, this book would not have been possible. There's not a day that goes by that I don't thank God for their health and happiness.

Family First – I'm grateful for the patience and support of my wife, Samantha, and our two beautiful daughters. Their understanding of my time away from them will hopefully give many other families and their children the opportunity to thrive in a new world forged by inclusive educational environments.

To my parents and my brother for providing an environment grounded in pragmatic education and safety of all children.

To all parents that so bravely navigate the incredible challenges of raising resilient children in an ever-complex educational world. The last 14 months within a pandemic have been unprecedently eye opening. The stories you have shared of your struggles are real and influenced the content of this book immensely.

Professionally – I have been extremely fortunate to work with so many amazing educators over the last twenty plus years. From first year teachers, fresh out of college to veteran administrators, you hold the key to a greater future. Our discussions, planning, and capital work are methodical instruments for change. Dr. Kevin McGowan, Lou Alaimo, Carlos Gildemeister, Jay Morris and so many others, thank you for your interest in the science of ABI and Sense-of-Place, and most importantly the follow through to make inclusive educational environments a reality. Dr. Marie Cianca and Dr. Shirley Green, thank you for giving context and breadth to a fledgling concept.

I have worked for many design firms during my career but none that can hold a candle to the desire to be innovative and provide meaningful design to that of SWBR. Phil Wise, Joe Gibbons, Tom Gears, and Dave Beinetti, thank you for your support, mentorship, and yearning to challenge the status quo.

Contents

Foreword 7

Prologue 9

Chapter 1: A Brief History of School Design and the Industrial Model of Education 12

Chapter 2: The Difference Between Traditional and Flexible Physical Learning Environments 21

Chapter 3: Emotional Intelligence: Are Students' Needs Evolving? 32

Chapter 4: Sense-of-Place: Does Physical Space Impact Our Ability to Learn? 45

Chapter 5: Equity and Inclusion: It's Time for a New Type of Leader to Emerge 60

Chapter 6: If It's So Important: Why Are We Not Evolving? 66

Chapter 7: A Recipe for Success: How You Can Be a Champion for Change 72

About the Author 79

References 81

Foreword

Dr. Joseph Kosiorek's book, ***Lost in Space: The Truth You Must Know to Enhance Student Engagement and Increase School Flexibility***, provides a tremendous chronological representation of how school buildings fail to meet the changing demands of teaching, learning, and student engagement. Dr. Kosiorek's proposed solutions are practical and realistic pathways to match structures with 21st-century curricula and teaching innovations.

Dr. Kosiorek's historical perspective on how school buildings have changed over the past 120 years reveals that while the contents of buildings have changed, the structures themselves have been slower to evolve. While the curriculum for students has dramatically changed, the next wave of educational innovation requires rethinking educational space. Dr. Kosiorek takes these complex issues and provides easy-to-understand insight into the development of proactive, practical learning environments. Dr. Kosiorek's book is excellent reading and inspiring visual work.

It is one thing to detail the history of school design; it is another to tie that process to the holistic needs of students and families. I appreciate that it rolls into key leadership endeavors that support the "whole learner" while clearly understanding that the school's physical structure is critical to support key determinants such as equity, inclusion, emotional intelligence, and sense of place. That focus is built on the understanding that school buildings are the center of the community is an assertion that is on target and powerful.

Dr. Kosiorek brings attention to support of learners and the flexibility to address unique learning in the future. ***Lost in Space*** serves as a roadmap for addressing the future of school design and how it will be essential to consider the unique needs of every child from a holistic perspective.

The future of school design – drivers and critical components:

Equity
Inclusion
Emotional Intelligence
Sense of Place

Anita Johnson,
Executive Director, National Center for Education Research and Technology

Prologue

This book is born out of many years of empirical research that uniquely and meaningfully fuses the professions of education and architecture. Yet this book is meant not only to educate but also to entertain. If education or knowledge is the destination, authentic engagement is the vehicle that gets you there.

As a parent, community member, PreK–12 educator, or an architect, we all play a role in the education our children receive. If you feel there is something wrong or outdated with the educational environment today, this book will help you define the issues. If you feel there is nothing wrong with today's educational environment, this book will offer a better understanding of why change is critical and provide foundational tools necessary to make meaningful improvements.

As parents, we try our best to provide our children with the skills of resiliency that prepare them for the challenges of life once they leave the nest. We try to enjoy the years before they do, while enduring the struggles of balancing all that life throws at us as adults. We try to advocate for our children so that they have the greatest breadth of opportunity to succeed while finding their way. How about the children without advocates? This book will help you understand why kids are falling through the cracks and how the educational environment can assist by closing that gap.

To be clear, this book is not a recipe and does not provide protocol for improving student test scores housed in a traditional rubric to pump out students like widgets in a factory; in fact, it is quite the opposite. As community members, you will walk away with a greater appreciation for the impact today's learning environments have on us all within the interwoven complexities of the local, national and even international economies.

Architects: please, please, please stop following the latest trends because they sound fun to say, the colors are vibrant, and the chairs wobble. A close educational colleague once said, "PreK–12 is highly susceptible to the flavor-of-the-week syndrome." Read this book because you want to understand why these trends may or may not be appropriate for a specific learning environment culture, or how they may work collectively to address the holistic and equitable needs of all learners.

As successful and innovative PreK–12 educators and administrators, novice and veteran, you will use the contents of this book as a reference manual, a weapon on your trajectory for change. Tab it, dogear pages, write notes in the margins, and please, by all means, challenge its contents. You are the gatekeepers of education, your craft, and you must be the tip of the spear. Rest assured, you are not alone, but if you accept this challenge, be prepared to face the status quo: it lurks around every corner and isn't giving up without a fight.

1

A Brief History of School Design and the Industrial Model of Education

School Daze

Think back for a moment, what was your most memorable experience in elementary school? For some, this was only a few years ago; for others it feels like a lifetime ago. No matter what the experience was or how fuzzy it may now be, do you remember where you were? You may be able to describe every detail of the environment that surrounded you, or nothing but the overall context of what it meant to you at the moment and what it means to you now. Why is that memory so valuable to the cortex of your brain, where long-term memories are stored away, like the kindergarten painting your mother held onto for years and then brought out the week you left for college! Some people are able to recall that experience as a purely cognitive event, some an emotional event, a social event, a physical event, or a combination of any or all four. This is called sense-of-place.

Sense-of-place is a perceived experience of a physical or cultural environment—an awareness that a person is part of a culture or community that is something greater than him- or herself. Sense of belonging, sense of community, sense of identity, and sense of self-worth are a few derivatives of the term. Sense-of-place is experienced through all five senses and is impacted by activities, meanings, individual features, and physical features (Falahat et al., 2017; Jalili & Azar, 2016). We'll dig deeper into the four sense-of-place components in Chapter 4.

Some of the greatest words of wisdom I ever received were on my wedding day. I don't recall if it was my mother or father—fuzzy memories! but they said, "During the events of the day, step back, and take a moment to appreciate everything around you." Sage and very simple advice. So simple: we have to be reminded to reflect on the moment, not after the day is done, but while still within the moment. Stepping back in the moment gives us the opportunity to appreciate, through all five senses, the environment that surrounds us.

As adults, we can reflect on that school age experience and now diagnose the learning environment via the four components of sense-of-place. As a child we could not, and at the time may have received the ruler for daydreaming, but as adults, it is our responsibility to provide opportunities that expand upon the experiences of our children through greater understanding and implementation of heathier environments by improving sense-of-place. So, let's get started by taking a trip down memory lane, not yours or mine but the systematic history of the educational learning environment.

The Traditional Learning Environment

If you were a young educator in 1880 in the United States, you most likely did not have formal education yourself. You had a wonderful group of approximately 10 to 30 neighborhood children of all ages in a one-room schoolhouse. Urban center industrialization streamlined the manufacturing process, putting many back to work, and you were elated that there was enough food on the table after a long depression. The assembly line was an amazing innovation. If it works for our financial economy, why couldn't it work for our educational or knowledge economy?

Fast forward to 1910, and you're now a seasoned educator. In your farming community, that one-room schoolhouse hasn't changed much since you started, but there are rumblings that in the city, schools are at the forefront of educational innovation by borrowing lessons learned from the successes of the assembly line. You're ready to pass your love for education down to your adult children. You had six siblings, none of them educators, so you are happy that one of your four children wants to continue in the family trade.

Your most inquisitive child ventured into the city to experience greener pastures on their own and to your delight has returned to the family farm to raise their own children and carry on the legacy: a love for education. They have seen what is called the "classroom," with children sitting in desks facing the front of the room focused on the teacher providing a lesson: not much different than what you and your children experienced with your own education in the one-room schoolhouse. But there's a difference: in these classrooms, all the children are of a similar age, and there are multiple classrooms closely connected by a corridor like a warehouse with rooms for each age group, a model used to address the overcrowding in the city. Your child raves about this model of efficiency.

Nothing much changes about the rural one-room schoolhouse until a depression of the likes you haven't seen since the 70s hits. It is the mid-1930s, and once again the lessons of industrialization create the opportunity for prosperity. Large township schools start popping up, replacing many one-room schoolhouses. Yours is still there and will be for another 20 years. Within your extended family of 30, six are out of work in these desparate times. They get back to work by pouring concrete, erecting steel, and laying the brick of the township school about a half mile down the road. It's an amazing feat of innovation, and finally your community has a brick building, three stories high, where most children in the community can come together and learn. Thank the heavens for the WPA (Works Progress Administration). The opportunities are endless: there is an indoor gymnasium, an auditorium, and indoor plumbing! By design, classrooms are separated from assembly spaces in a school to industrialize the learning process by the elimination of distraction (Baker, 2012). Classrooms are the physical learning environments where reading, writing, science, and mathematics are taught as the skills most desired for successful jobs in the soon-to-be reinvigorated manufacturing economy.

As the urban and township model for educational environments both physically and pedagogically fully embrace the industrial design model through the 1940s, 50s and 60s to meet the demands of the financial economy, the bifurcation of the knowledge economy begins to take shape. The socialized methods that banded us together to wage war, both actual and economic begin to yield to individualism. By the late 60s and early 70s, educators yearning to instill the values of a well-balanced learner push up against the establishment. Movements for equality and environmental sustainability are taking shape, and the most innovative of educators want their learning environments to reflect these values. A valiant effort to disrupt the traditional, industrial educational model that has been in place for almost a century now, using an open classroom floor plan model, is fleeting by the 1980s; educational pedagogies return to a rote memorization, teacher-centered model. Educational space recedes to the classroom and corridor model, that would later be referred to as, "Cells and Bells," indicating that the school bell rings, and students exit a classroom (cell) into a corridor. The next bell rings, and the students vacate the corridor to enter their next classroom (Nair, 2014). In Chapter 3 we'll get into more detail about why the 1970s open classroom failed so miserably, but now on to the 80s.

The 1980s brought with it an innovation that would change everything, or so we thought. With the advent of the personal computer, workplace design shifted to meet the evolving needs of most professional environments. Between 1990 and 2019, the average physical workplace environment increased communal space from 15% to 40% (Schittich, 2011). Largely because of the personal computer, workplace designs needed to provide environments that supported fewer routine processes and were increasingly adaptable and flexible to change. Our manufacturing economy was evolving into a service economy. Flexible workplace spaces were engaging and cognizant of employees' sense-of-place needs. Flexible and creative workplace environments met the needs of business and cultural models that require collaboration, engagement, and creativity. Personal or individual workspaces requiring reflection and introspective opportunities were included in flexible workplace design, but they were becoming limited, compared to the traditional office design model by the 2000s.

So here we are in the 2020s. The U.S. workplace environment has fully evolved from agricultural, to manufacturing, and now to a service economy, all in less than 150 years. The economy will evolve ever more rapidly with technology and artificial intelligence creating a connected global workplace. And where is the educational environment? Still stubbornly holding on to the innovations of the assembly line, the industrial model, in physical space and in the learning model.

School Days Revisited

Now ask yourself that question again, but this time not, what, but where was your most memorable experience in elementary school? Was it in a classroom, in the gymnasium, the locker room, in a hallway, or on the staircase between classes? The most impactful learning experiences happen in a variety of physical environments, yet the classroom has traditionally been regarded as the most identifiable place for basic formal learning (Bekerman et al., 2006). But was the formal learning experience what made the greatest life-learning impression on you today?

Traditional physical learning environments do one great thing: promote compliance and assimilation (Parsons, 2017). These skills are still very much needed in today's workplace, in the formal spaces, the conference rooms, but now need to be complemented by creativity, autonomy, and self-regulation. These are the skills that are increasingly required by employers today (Jerald, 2009). Such skills include creativity/innovation, ethics/social responsibility, critical thinking/problem solving, and collaboration. These skills combine a variety of areas of study, and they are in sharp contrast to what was required by employers prior to the introduction of personal computing in the 1980s. In-demand skills, prior to the introduction of the personal computer, included the singularly taught subjects: the humanities/arts, history/geography, government/economics, foreign languages, the sciences, and mathematics. Singularly taught subjects and cognitive skills are supported by traditional classroom design because of their ability to promote compliance and assimilation. In the workplace, these spaces are designed for concentration with limited distraction, and they take the form of individual offices and meeting rooms. Traditional physical learning environments are cellular or modularly designed, and they fulfill personal and territorial behavioral needs. Does that describe the majority of classrooms in your school district? If you're saying "yes right now, keep reading!

So Where Do We Go From Here?

If traditional PreK–12 physical learning environments, alone, no longer support the teaching of the skills that are most sought after by employers, where do we go from here? More space was the historical and traditional answer to increased-learning environment needs. Bolt on a couple of boxes, I mean classrooms, to an existing wing, and let's call it a day! Sadly, that has been the model for enrollment fluctuations for far too long—since the 1950s, to be more specific.

More recently, the shift to a student-centered learning environment, desired by innovative and proactive educators, has unfortunately and misguidedly resulted in stuffing technology and a variety of furniture types into a box, the existing traditional physical learning environment.

Sorry, techies and interior designers: round peg, square classroom, a band-aid attempt for a much larger challenge.

A wise person once said, "Let's get physical!" Olivia Newton John wasn't wrong. In fact, let's extend it: not only physical, but let's get flexible physical learning environments. In Chapter 2, we'll discuss the difference between traditional physical learning environments and flexible physical learning environments, and how they impact our ability to learn and thrive as collaborative members of a community in this evolving knowledge economy.

Chapter Summary

1. Authentic engagement provides opportunities for children to be more resilient.
2. Sense-of-place is the vehicle used to achieve authentic engagement.
3. The financial economy over the last 150 years has evolved bringing with it innovations of the knowledge economy and workplace environment needs and design.
4. The educational environment, both physical and pedagogical, has not adapted.
5. With all five senses, reflect on your most impactful educational experience: the one, or maybe two that propelled you on a path that helped craft who you are today. Did it take place in the classroom, where you spent approximately two-thirds of your school day?

2

The Difference Between Traditional and Flexible Physical Learning Environments

On a fall morning in the mid 1980s in a small upstate New York town there sits a two-story 1950s vintage brick K–8 elementary school. The building houses one classroom per grade level. From the outside, the building is U shaped, facing due north. There are double doors at each end of the top of the U that face a large blacktop parking lot. There is a small grassy area tucked inside the U where no more than two single family houses could fit, no back yards included, less than a half-acre. In the middle of that grassy area is a flag pole.

On the inside, split level down the steps to the first floor, toilet rooms and the kitchen are to the left, while the cafetorium takes up the rest of the first floor with the exception of the kindergarten classroom and the gymnasium at the other end of the U. The floor is brown and white vinyl tile, and the walls are cream colored, smooth, and shiny structural glazed block 10 courses high. Walk up the switchback stairs to the second floor, same floor tile, same wall block. To the left is the first-grade classroom, then the main office. Keep walking down the hall, the next door on the left is the second-grade classroom. Turn the corner of the U, same floor tile, same wall block. The hallway is narrow; there are no lockers; that cream colored structural glazed block, 10 courses high, starts to create a cavernous feel. Doors alternate down either side of the hall. There is no one in the hall because class is in session, with the exception of one third grader in an adjoined desk-chair tucked closely to that cold, shiny, cream-colored block outside the third-grade classroom door, the first door in the long hallway to the right.

This boy in a white collared button-up shirt, snap-on blue tie, blue corduroys, and black shoes is out in the hallway because he finds it challenging to work independently. If you were to open the door to the classroom, you would see wooden cubbies to the left, a black chalkboard to the right. The teacher's heavy green steel desk sits in front of the chalkboard. There is a bank of windows in front of you the entire length on the rectangular room. Under those windows is a radiant heating vent and a sill-height counter with shelves of textbooks below. To the left at the back of the room there is more storage for projects and crafts. In the middle of the room, facing the chalkboard, sit approximately 20 neatly aligned adjoined desk-chairs with the flip top for students to store their pencils, textbooks wrapped in grocery bag paper, and trapper keepers. Those desks and the students in them don't move from their positions all year long. The walls are covered with a proud teacher's favorite educational graphics of historic figures, cursive handwritten letters, and a mural-size roll-up projection screen world map. The classroom floors are the same brown and white vinyl tile; the walls, pitted concrete block; the ceiling, a 2-foot by 4-foot tile grid with fluorescent lighting.

A singular subject, one after another, is the focus of successive 40-minute period after 40-minute period that changes at the ring of the bell. Does this ring any bells? It should; this is what we call the *traditional physical learning environment.* No wonder we were so eager to go to lunch, recess, computer classroom, the library, or the gymnasium, anything that stimulated the senses. Do you remember any of your classmates refusing to go to lunch because they were so engaged after 40 minutes of sitting in that hard desk memorizing fact after fact? I don't remember that ever happening either!

Now, back to that young boy in the hallway during the second period, on a fall day in the mid 1980s, in a small upstate New York town, in a small two-story brick 1950s vintage K–8 elementary school. The initial sting of being asked by the teacher to remove himself from the classroom has quickly worn off, and he gets down to the rote task workbook assignment without distraction, the same assignment that all the other 19 children are doing within the classroom. He works distraction free until about halfway through the period, when Sister Mary Hughes turns the corner from the main office and walks toward the boy. Anxiety builds in the boy, as he knows Sister Mary Hughes, a very intimidating presence, is about to approach him. She does not approach him, crisis evaded. Sister Mary Hughes, whom most of the boys in third grade call Sister Huggies, continues to walk down that long ominous hallway. As she is about to turn the next corner in the U, far enough away that it would be difficult for you to make out the top letter of an eye exam chart, a loud shriek echoes from the opposite length of the building near where the young boy in the hallway is sitting, back faced to Sister Mary Hughes' position. Sister Mary Hughes quickly pivots in her gray orthotics and begins her long march back down the lengthy hallway toward the boy.

No one else is in the hallway but the young boy and an increasingly aggravated Sister Mary Hughes picking up speed towards the boy. The boy gets smaller in his chair as the footsteps become louder and louder, reverberating off of those hard, cold, shiny, cream-colored block wainscot walls. Sister Mary Hughes finally arrives at her destination, towering over the boy, red with fury, and begins to give him the riot act about the inappropriateness of outbursts and the lack of respect. Obviously, the boy is acting out in retaliation for his teacher's punitive action, removing him from the classroom to separate the disruptor from the herd. The boy cowers at first, as the spit flies from Sister Mary Hughes' oral damnation. But then the boy sits up straight with half confidence, claims it wasn't him and begs her to believe him. Sister Mary Hughes is insistent that it was the boy; who else could it be? The boy maintains his innocence as a cross-armed Sister Mary Hughes struggles with the situation. This goes on for what must feel like five minutes to the boy, but in reality, the exchange is only about 30 seconds, during which the same shriek is heard again. Still, Sister Mary Hughes and the boy are the only two in the hallway until a toddler barrels around the corner; in hot pursuit is the mother. The mother scoops up her child and apologizes to Sister Mary Hughes for the disruption, then heads back into the main office and closes the door behind her.

You could hear a pin drop in the hallway now. Sister Mary Hughes takes a deep breath. In a very authoritative voice, keeping her erect posture and looking down at the boy, she apologizes in the most authentic way an affectless adult can. She then pivots and continues in the opposite direction down the hallway to complete the mission she began before what was, to her, this nonevent with the third-grader in the hallway. Sister Mary Hughes and the boy never had semblance of a meaningful conversation after that day, but that wasn't a bad thing. Future reprimands of the boy coming from Sister Mary Hughes had a much different tone. If you haven't figured it out by now, that boy was this author. That is my most memorable experience in elementary school.

Don't be concerned if your elementary school memory isn't as vivid, down to the color of the walls. Do take this opportunity to use all five senses to conjure up a few more details of your memory: the sounds—distracting or focusing, the smells—pleasant or off-putting, the feel—physical or emotional. This detailing exercise will prove to be the parts that collectively create your sense-of-place whole.

The Traditional Learning Environment (School Daze) Re-revisited

Let's break that memory down in terms of the learning environment. Obviously, it has all the hallmark characteristics of a traditional learning environment. If you're starting to break it down based on the historic longevity of traditional learning environments and disagree, go back to your highlighted text and margin notes from Chapter 1. This memory takes place in a traditional learning environment, both physically and pedagogically. Let's start with the traditional pedagogical learning environment:

1. The hallway is not a learning area, but sometimes used to rid the class of disruption; education only happened in the classroom space.
2. Singular subjects are taught and transition to the next subject by the ringing of a bell.
3. Workbooks are a staple for rote memorization; the same assignment is given to all students.
4. Assigned seating.

5. The classroom is a teacher's domain, teacher-centered, making control possible.

Now granted, this is a stark example. In the 35 plus years since, educators have done an amazing job evolving their pedagogy with limited support. But the facts above remain in 67% of learning environments in the United States, according to a 2015 study by the Education Week Research Center.

The traditional pedagogical learning environment is supported by the traditional physical learning environment. Now let's look at the aspects of a traditional physical learning environment:

1. Durable, yet monotonous and often institutional floor and wall finishes.
2. Long, narrow, straight, hallways connecting rectangular classroom after classroom of the same size on either side.
3. Classrooms remote from other types of spaces.
4. A well-established front of room.
5. Static classroom furniture and storage.

How Does This Differ From the Flexible Learning Environment?

Pedagogically, a flexible learning environment is exactly that, flexible:

1. More often than not, a flexible or block schedule is required to provide student-centered, personalized learning experiences.

2. Student groupings of varying sizes are used, not just your typical classroom of 16–24 broken down into four or five student groups, but transdisciplinary student groupings of 96, 48, 24, 12, 6, and 3.
3. Project-based learning (PBL) activities within a real-life context are used and supported by technology.
4. The learning environment belongs to all and is there to serve students' needs.

While a traditional pedagogy alone is adequately supported by a traditional physical learning environment, only a flexible physical learning environment can support both traditional and flexible pedagogical learning. That is because the flexible physical learning environment is inclusive of traditional learning environments. A successful physical learning environment includes three interconnected or networked physical learning environment space types: F-Space (Formal Space), S-Space (Social Learning Space), and C-Space (Creative Space) (Jankowska & Atlay, 2008). Academic physical learning environment types can be directly linked to workplace physical environments via sense-of-place phenomenology, or perceived experience.

1. Formal Spaces or F-Space:

    The traditional physical learning environment or F-Space is the academic equivalent of the boardroom. The traditional physical learning environments dominated PreK–12 design for 150 years, and they are teacher-centered. In academia, these spaces are for seminars and lectures. In the workplace, F-Spaces are designed for concentration with limited distraction, and they take the form of individual offices and meeting rooms. Traditional physical learning environments are cellular or modularly designed, and they fulfill personal and territorial behavioral needs, student and teacher, or employer and employee.

2. Social Learning Spaces or S-Space:

    S-spaces are the informal spaces that connect traditional learning environments. They are the transition spaces, or the spaces between the spaces where informal conversations happen, such as the ad-hoc conversation between a teacher and student in the corridor or courtyard. In the workplace, these spaces are designed for movement and communication, and they take the form of the kitchenette, lounge, printer station, touch down workstations for visiting staff from other offices, and filing or archive areas.

3. Creative Spaces or C-Space:

    C-Spaces encourage creativity. Unlike F-Space, C-Space is designed for exploration and reconfiguration, using movable or flexible partitions, furniture, and technology; variations of patterns and textures; and writable surfaces. C-Space encourages critical-thinking and problem-solving skills. These academic spaces are student-centered, where the educator acts as a facilitator in lieu of acting as an instructor. In the workplace, these spaces are for collaboration and the exchange of ideas. C-Spaces include think-tank space, project areas, and medium-to-small group meeting places.

Many empirical studies either support or expand upon this fundamental three interconnected space-type model and its impact on student and educator sense-of-place. Now we have a better understanding of the pedagogical and physical differences between traditional learning environments and flexible learning environments. We also understand, from Chapter 1, the historical context of how we arrived at this place—from the one-room schoolhouse, to the industrial model, to that epic failure of the open classroom of the 1970s, and back to the industrial model in the 1980s, which is very much still alive now.

In Figure 2.1, from left to right, the PreK–12 Physical Learning Environment Pendulum has swung from traditional, to non-traditional, back to traditional and is now making its way back to the center. It is human nature to overshoot, overcompensate, and overreact in either direction, as was the case with the violent swing form traditional space, to the open classroom, and the inevitable retreat to the traditional in the 1980s. We learned in this chapter that flexible is NOT open, flexible is NOT closed: flexible is a combination of connected size and type spaces. Flexible physical learning environments are the pendulum at rest, an equilibrium.

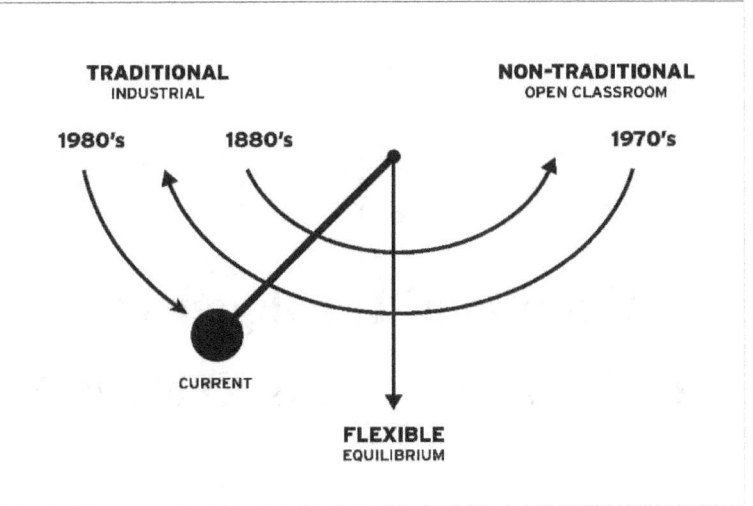

Figure 2.1. The Learning Space Pendulum Swing.

In Chapter 3 we will examine how traditional and flexible physical learning environments impact learning differently, and why it is critical to address student emotional intelligence needs.

3

Emotional Intelligence:
Are Students' Needs Evolving?

When noted educational researcher Craig Jerald provided and published "Defining a 21st Century Education" for the Center for Public Education in 2009, he addressed three areas of learning, critical for success: (a) Traditional Skills, (b) Real World, or Applied Literacy Skills, and (c) Broader Competencies. First, the traditional skills of Math, Reading, and Writing will always be at the core of learning, as they have been for centuries. Second, he emphasized the applied literacy skills required to synthesize or translate traditional skills applicable to real world scenarios. Lastly, he explained the broader competencies, the employer desired emotional intelligence skills of creativity/innovation, ethics/social responsibility, critical thinking/problem solving, and collaboration that we discussed in Chapter 1. These three learning areas for success are supported by the three space types discussed in Chapter 2.

Combined, these three areas of learning and three types of physical environments create a sense-of-place, an awareness by their occupants that they are part of a culture, a community, something greater than themselves. Lin and Lockwood (2014) referred to this awareness as personal identity. They also referred to emotional attachment to a physical space as place identity. Emotional bonds are created and recreated by individuals during engagement and reengagement of physical spaces and places (Lengen & Kistemann, 2012). Awareness of emotional bonds, and the ability to regulate or adapt emotion to a space and fellow space users, is defined as emotional intelligence (Uzzaman & Karim, 2018). Emotional intelligence and sense-of-place are, therefore, closely linked and are impacted by the spatial elements of flexible physical learning environments.

PBL and LCP impact on Emotional Intelligence

Employer-valued skills of creativity/innovation, ethics/social responsibility, critical thinking/problem solving, and collaboration require emotional intelligence. Emotional intelligence skills are fostered by participatory learning environments (Landau & Meirovich, 2011). In addition, emotional intelligence skills are positively affected by PBL instruction methods (Ahlfeldt et al., 2005). Figure 3.1 shows that average student retention rates are higher using participatory learning environment methods that encourage teamwork, peer-to-peer, and student-to-educator interaction.

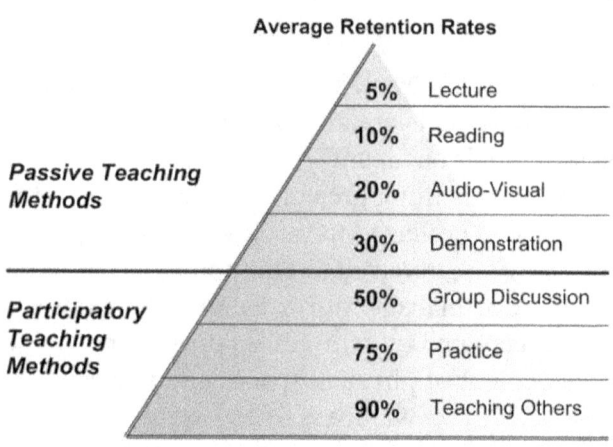

*Adapted from National Training Laboratories. Bethel, Maine

Figure 3.1. Average Student Retention Rates. Adapted from "Learning Pyramid," (2018) National Training Laboratories Institute

Judith Meece (2003) defined the learner-centered practices (LCPs) education model by five characteristics. First, learners are unique and must take responsibility for engaging in their learning. Second, learners have unique learning rates, emotional states of mind, abilities, and talents. Cedar Riener and Daniel Willingham (2010) similarly described these characteristics as learning preferences. Third, learning happens best when the subject is meaningful to the learner. Fourth, learning occurs best in a safe, supportive, and comfortable environment. Fifths, learners are interested in mastering their own world.

Successful participatory learning and PBL environments require that students perceive their educational environments to be supportive and safe (Landau & Meirovich, 2011). It is a challenge within traditional learning environments to address and support multiple student learning styles. Student learning styles have been defined by the VARK model: visual, aural, reading, and kinesthetic (Othman & Amiruddin, 2010). Individuals who are visual learners are most comfortable when taught with graphics and illustration. Aural learners thrive when given verbal instruction. Reading learners excel by reading the written word, and kinesthetic learners prefer experiential or hands-on learning and physical movement.

Know Your ABIs

Although student learning style theory has mainstream appeal, Riener and Willingham (2010) argued that there is no evidence to support that so-called visual learners perform better or are more engaged if they are presented with information in graphic form. The same holds true for so-called aural, reading, and kinesthetic learners. Rather, they defined a variety of individual student learning preferences based on genetic differences, ability and interests, background knowledge, and learning disabilities.

A simplified adaption of student learning preferences can be defined as ABI. *ABI* represents the three learner extents or senses that influence student engagement and capacity to learn different areas of content based on: (a) Ability—The genetic differences or individual innate qualities; (b) Background—The knowledge or fundamental skills that promote learning secondary skills within similar content; and (c) Interests—The activities that pique individual curiosities. When you address and understand an individual student's ABI, the barriers to authentic engagement can be removed.

Now, take a moment to define your own ABI:

A – Ability: What came naturally to you when you were young? Did you naturally enjoy picking up a book and reading to yourself, or maybe reading to others? Were you in the pool for hours every day of the summer because your physical attributes just allowed you to glide through the water faster than all the kids in your neighborhood? Were your parents educators, or did they play a sport in college or professionally? These innate qualities or strengths played a large role in your life's trajectorial path. Malcolm Gladwell (2013) went as far to say that the time of year you were born influences your statistical chances of becoming a professional hockey player.

B – Background: Your worldview has been crafted by the time and place in which you grew up, your socioeconomic status, and the fundamental skills that were presented to you in your developmental years. Did you build a treehouse with your father or mother? Was there something always cooking in the kitchen, and a family member took the time to share their love for the culinary arts? Was there a bookcase in the living room that stretched a mile high where a relative would always perch, nearby, during the holidays, eager to reveal to you the wonderful journeys that could be taken without leaving the house. Your background, cultural framework, and all the unique skills that collectively create your whole, explicitly—but more likely, implicitly—built on your natural abilities and combined, influenced your interests.

I – Interests: Interests began to take shape after your abilities and background created a foundation sturdy enough to allow you to dip your toes in unfamiliar waters. Kenneth Ginsburg and (2011) could support that the toe-dip only becomes wading in the water waist-high, or eventually diving head-first into a specific interest, once a child feels their A and B have been positively reinforced. Resilience is the currency that buys the opportunity to explore greater depth and breadth of interests. Did you take that ability to swim laps around the neighborhood kids to the next level, pushing yourself with an interest to be faster than everyone in your school? Did you take that family tradition of cooking to explore and fuse multiple ethnic dishes that everyone in your social circle couldn't get enough of? Once that interest becomes a passion, and that passion can be monetized, that ABI becomes an opportunity for a scholarship, a potential career path, or a lifelong fitness regimen. This is where Meece's LCP characteristics three and five play such a formative role in a child's development, projecting, *"meaning"* and, *"mastery of their own world"* into their curriculum.

If you're an educator, take a moment to define your students' ABI. Chances are you've been able to increase one or more of your students' engagement through nontraditional means. That standoffish child just has a different ABI. What approach can you take, what rabbit hole do you need to climb down to coax that learner out of their proverbial corner? Now, could the physical environment have aided you in your efforts? Could Meece's LCP characteristic number four be supported by the physical environment that is inclusive of all, yet at the same time, *"safe and comfortable"* in a time of individual or small group needs?

We'll also talk about ABI more in Chapter 5, when we discuss and define the future of equitable and inclusive educational environments.

Back to LCP

In traditional learning environments, some students choose not to participate because of the fear of rejection. Other students dominate conversations, reducing others' ability to participate (Landau & Meirovich, 2011). In some cases, students are separated into smaller groups outside of the traditional classroom to create a participatory learning environment that meets individual student learning preferences, their ABI.

Some of Meece's research involved administering the Assessment of Learner-Centered Practices (ALCP) survey to 109 teachers and 2,200 middle school students from urban, suburban, and rural schools across the United States. The purpose of the survey was to assess learner-centered teaching practices with three goals: mastery, performance, and work avoidance.

LCP Impact on Students

Research results show LCP had the strongest positive association with student motivation, achievement, and mastery. Learner-centered teaching practices had a greater impact on mastery than did class size or teacher experience. Positive impact on performance was also realized. Work avoidance was negatively correlated to learner-centered teaching practices. Students became less focused on avoiding work when learner-centered teaching practices included adaptive and personalized instruction, caring, respecting the student voice, and instilling higher order thinking.

LCP Impact on Educators

Irene White and Francesca Lorenzi (2016) referred to these qualities as being, emotionally supportive environments to succeed. The most interesting result of Meece's study was that students rated educators as more effective when using LCP. She also defined the educator's role in learner-centered classrooms by providing the students with opportunities to choose, opportunities for collaboration, a variety of instructional strategies, activities that were relevant, facilitation, and a sense of belonging or sense-of-place. LCP empower students, and at the same time, they increase teacher perceived classroom performance.

Back to PBL

In a survey of 62,000 college students, using the Student Engagement (SE) Survey based on the 2000 National Survey of Student Engagement (NSSE) Report about learning environments, researchers set out to understand how PBL impacts student engagement. The study revealed that classes with higher PBL levels had an average engagement score (ES) equal to or higher than the NSSE national average. As course level increased, engagement increased; as class enrollment decreased, engagement increased; and as PBL increased, engagement increased. Most interestingly, PBL teaching methods provided in large classrooms also had a substantial positive impact on student engagement. This finding has important implications for educators' perception that a smaller number of students is required to provide successful PBL methods. Therefore, it's not class size, *enrollment*, or singular class size, *space*, that impacts engagement; it is the ability to create a variety of sized student groupings in a variety of sized spaces that is most effective at increasing authentic student engagement.

Connecting Engagement to Achievement

The 2015 Gallup Student Poll Survey (Gallup, Inc., 2016), including of approximately one million students in the United States, concluded that students' perceived engagement level dropped off significantly from Grade 5 to Grade 11. The most significant drop, 67% for Grade 5 to 37% for Grade 11, was in response to agree or disagree with the following statement, "The adults at my school care about me" (Gallup, Inc., 2016, p. 7). What is causing this perceived lack of belonging, personal identity, and sense-of-place?

PBL methods and participatory classroom environments are both nontraditional teaching and learning methods. How do participatory classroom environments impact emotional intelligence development, and is emotional intelligence connected to academic achievement? Gavriel Meirovich (Landau & Meirovich, 2011), an ethics and organizational behavior expert, studied both. Employers are increasingly seeking strong soft skills or emotional intelligence, yet they continue to be dissatisfied with recent graduates' competence in this area. Meirovich described emotional intelligence as measured by the 141-item online Mayer-Salovey-Caruso Emotional Intelligence Test (MSCEIT), which has four categories: (a) accurate perception of emotions, self, and others; (b) facilitate through using emotions; (c) understanding connections between emotions that differ; and (d) managing emotions, self, and others.

The MSCEIT was performed to test the participatory classroom environment's impact on emotional intelligence development and emotional intelligence connections to academic achievement. Results support that there is a positive correlation between participatory classroom environments and emotional intelligence. There was no link between emotional intelligence and academic achievement in terms of grade point average (GPA).

Most interestingly, women and students with more full-time work experience had higher emotional intelligence. This finding makes two important connections: first, gender plays a role in providing learning environment equity; and second, greater levels of emotional intelligence are required by the workplace than are generally provided by traditional learning environments.

Plainly said, if increasing GPA—academic achievement— is your only goal, traditional learning environments have outperformed and will continue to consistently outperform. If your only goal is to increase emotional intelligence, emotional intelligence skills, nontraditional learning environments outperform traditional learning environments. If your goal is to provide equitable opportunities to foster both student cognitive and emotional intelligence skills, it's time to start looking more seriously at flexible learning environments.

Chapter Summary

1. Data support student engagement and emotional intelligence's role in creating a sense-of-place.
2. Student engagement and emotional intelligence, stimulating a variety of individual student learning preferences, ABI, and students' sense-of-place have shown to be successful in educational environments that provide LCP, PBL instruction methods, and participatory learning methods.
3. Innovative, creative, student-centered pedagogies need to be as diverse as the students that the pedagogies serve.
4. There is no one-size-fits-all solution to creating a learning environment that supports the development of student emotional intelligence, engagement, and sense-of-place.

Easy as 1, 2, 3—Chapters 1, 2, and 3, That Is

Now we know **HOW** we got here—the history of the learning environment, **WHAT** the differences are—among traditional, nontraditional, and flexible learning environments, and **WHY** flexible teaching methods and learning preferences are so important—LCP and PBL that address emotional intelligence through student ABI.

How – Historically speaking, why do we continually fail to provide spaces that support equitable learning environments? Well, we continue to treat technology as a special like we did in the 1980s. It's not; technology is now a mode of communication and an open information-gathering highway or journey, no longer an isolated destination. We have come a long way since then, but dedicated computer classrooms still exist, retrofitted, by reason of analogy to the keyboarding space. PBL is not a special either; it's a framework. Yet we continue to bolt STEM (Science, Technology, Engineering, and Math) additions onto the end of traditional classroom and corridor model, school building wings. The 1970s open classroom was an innovative attempt to incorporate PBL, but unfortunately it was missing two essential ingredients: technology, and variety of space; bad timing, as we have both now.

Why – So why do we, as PreK–12 educators and administrators, architects, and community members, insist on treating technology and student-centered PBL as a special? Because we don't have the space to decentralize education appropriately and effectively.

What – Now it's time to fuse learning/pedagogy with space!

4

Sense-of-Place:
Does Physical Space Impact Our Ability to Learn?

Linking academic and workplace physical environments via sense-of-place is important to the lifelong learning and workforce development processes (Schittich, 2011). Sense-of-place and student engagement are connected. Student engagement can be defined in terms of attendance, learning, and motivation (Adedokun et al., 2017). Sense-of-place should not be confused with student achievement or outcomes. The 2015 Brown Center Report on American Education (Loveless, 2015) and the Program for International Student Assessment (National Center for Education Statistics (NCES, 2015) indicate that measuring students' sense-of-place and engagement differs from state to state in the United States and from country to country, worldwide. For these reasons, it is important that creating positive sense-of-place, not student outcomes, is the barometer for measuring successful PreK–12 flexible learning environments to address a variety of student learning preferences, ABI.

Sense-of-Place

Sense-of-place is a perceived experience of a physical or cultural environment. An awareness that a person is part of a culture or community that is something greater than him- or herself. Sense of belonging, sense of community, sense of identity, and sense of self-worth are a few derivatives of the term. Sense-of-place is experienced through all five senses and is impacted by activities, meanings, individual features, and physical features (Falahat et al., 2017; Jalili & Azar, 2016). Sense-of-place is an expansion of Barker's (1968) behavior-setting theory and its connection to the environment, to ecology, to the community, and to sociology by including activities and meaning categories from psychology (Georgiou et al., 1996; Popov & Chompalov, 2012; Proshansky et al., 1976; Scott, 2005). Barker's behavior-setting theory has two parts: place and behavior patterns. Place is defined as the surroundings inhabited by a person, whether they be physical or cultural. Behavior patterns are defined as the physical act of doing something, of completing a task. The sense-of-place framework's inclusion of activities and meanings provides a comprehensive and effective framework for assessing PreK–12 learning environments. Let's now break down the four characteristics of the Sense-of-Place Framework.

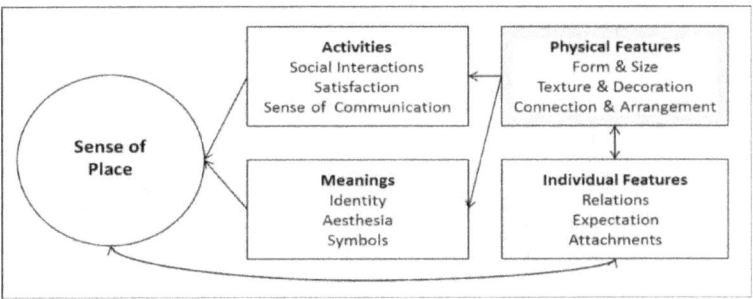

Figure 4.1. Sense-of-Place Model. Adapted from "The Sense-of-Place and Its Factors," by M. A. Falahat, 2006

Activities

Activities are described as social interactions, satisfaction, and sense of community. The activity of social interactions between peer students, mentors, educators, and staff have direct influence on sense-of-place. Activities, understood through traditions and formality, or being foreign as a first-time experience, impact the comfort of an environment. An individual's or group's satisfaction with these activities and pedagogies elicits either positive or negative responses. The freedom to communicate through verbal and body language determines connectivity or separation. Traditional teaching practices of a teacher-centered model cannot be successful in a flexible physical learning environment, which was demonstrated in the failed open classroom model of the 1970s in the United States. The student-centered model allows for the expansion of pedagogy.

Meanings

Meanings are described as identity, aesthesia, and symbols. Meanings are the symbolic gestures that make up an organizational culture through mission, vision, and goals. A group identifies with a common understanding of what they stand for and what they are trying to accomplish as a group. Aesthesia, or the ability to perceive sensations via physical or metaphoric symbology, also determines physical and/or emotional connectivity or separation.

Individual Features

Individual features are closely linked to physical features and can be described through relations, expectation, and attachments. Scale and its relationship to the human proportion, as a child or adult, influence an environment's impact on sense-of-place via the individual features through individual perception. That perception is different between children and adults (Jalili & Azar, 2016). The expectation or lack of expectation determines behavior and the recovery of desired behavior. There is a level of attachment to expectation and, conversely, to change (Vali & Nasekhiyan, 2014). We'll discuss the power of the status quo, and how change management facilitates growth in Chapters 6 and 7.

Physical Features

Sense-of-place physical features can be defined as learning environment architectural design elements. Collaborative learning, physical comfort, instructor-student interactions, and student-student interactions are four criteria to gauge sense-of-place (Adedokun et al., 2017). These four criteria are impacted by physical features described as form and size, texture and decoration, and connection and arrangement.

Using the Sense-of-Place Framework, you are now able to distill any PreK–12 district or organization into four quantifiable components to determine if it is a successfully engaging environment. Refer to Figure 4.1 on page 47. In more simplified terms, we understand that PreK–12 administrators and educators play approximately a 75% role in setting the tone of the organization through: (a) *Activities*, traditions, and formalities, (b) *Meanings*, mission, vision, and goals, and (c) *Individual Features*, setting a level of expectation for behavior. The remaining 25%, and the much overlooked fourth piece to the puzzle for organizational success, is *Physical Features*: space that creates safe and engaging opportunities to support cultural and pedagogical needs, the first three areas above. You can use the following equation with respect to your own PreK–12 district or organization:

$$(E \times 3) + PE = SOP$$

$$\text{Aka} - E3PE$$

E x 3 or E3 = Three pedagogical or learning environments: Activities, Meanings, and Individual Features

PE = Physical Environment: physical features and spatial elements

SOP = Sense-of-Place

Are you a teacher or administrator, early in your career, interviewing for a position at a new district or PreK–12 organization? Ask the interviewer what traditions they have: how do they live through their mission or strategic plan? What are their goals? Will your role be seen as a cultural fit or a cultural add? The two are starkly different if an organization has goals for maintenance, or goals for growth and change.

Are you a veteran teacher or a seasoned administrator at the top of your game? Student outcomes are consistently high, but you sense that your organization lacks equity and inclusion. Maybe it's time to evaluate engagement and how the physical environment supports sense-of-place.

Did or do your children attend the district or PreK–12 organization within your community that seems to have a singular vision for pathways to higher education? Not all student ABIs require a four-year degree. Now may be the time to assess engagement in your educational community and how the elements of sense-of-place are valued.

If 2 parts hydrogen and 1 part oxygen are required to sustain life on Earth, E3PE is required for the future of sustainable education. Traditional learning environments alone are suffocating student engagement, emotional intelligence, and cognitive innovation. The survival of our financial economy and our thought economy depend on this change toward equitable and sustainable learning environments through the sense-of-place lens.

What Flexible Physical (Space) Learning Environments Offer That Traditional Do Not

Remember the fundamental three interconnected space type model from Chapter 2: F-Space (Formal Space); S-Space (Social Learning Space), and C-Space (Creative Space)? Let's break down the physical elements of each space type and how they impact learning. There are three elements within each of these three interconnected space types that create a successful flexible physical learning environment: technology, furniture, and most importantly the variety of space size and type.

Formal Spaces or F-Space

The traditional physical learning environment or F-Space is commonly referred to as the classroom, the workplace equivalent of the boardroom. We know the most about this space type because it has been in use for the last 150 years; is a constant, not having changed much since; and continues to be the most commonly used learning environment today. F-Spaces are designed for concentration with limited distraction. Cognitive learning, rote memorization, the teacher-centered model, and achievement have been proven to flourish in this environment. Traditional physical learning environments are cellular or modularly designed, and they fulfill personal and territorial behavioral needs of both student and teacher. We thoroughly defined one example of the physical elements of the traditional physical learning environment, within its historical context in Chapter 2. Therefore, we won't redefine F-Space here, but we will use it as the benchmark to define both S-Space and C-Space. Take the time to go back to Chapter 2 and review your traditional learning environment margin notes if you have set the book down between chapters for some time.

During the last 30 years, technology and furniture have evolved immensely. Unfortunately, they have both been misused—or rather, misplaced. We continue to try and fit a round peg in a square hole. That is, we continue to stuff iPads, multiple computer screens, reconfigurable tables, wobble chairs, standing desks, etc., in a traditional classroom box, and viola, Flexible Classroom. Flexible Classroom is an oxymoron; there is no such thing.

Classrooms serve the purpose we described, designed for concentration with limited distraction. We need these spaces, so stop trying to put lipstick on a pig. This misuse of space happens for many reasons that we will discuss in detail in Chapter 6. The greatest reason for this misuse of space is the lack of complementary and connected variety of space types that more appropriately and effectively use decentralized technology and flexible furniture.

Social Learning Spaces or S-Space

S-spaces are the informal spaces that connect traditional learning environments. They are the transition spaces, or the spaces between the spaces, where informal conversations happen, such as the ad-hoc conversation between a teacher and student in the corridor or courtyard. Courtyard and corridor are unfortunately the predominant limitations of space in most existing PreK–12 physical learning environment building configurations that represent S-Space. Often, educators desire S-Space and by default, move small groupings of students into the corridor to satisfy this need and break out from the traditional setting. Either that, or a teacher must trek their students halfway across the building, in a centralized model, to a space that accommodates this need, making it infeasible to create multiple student groupings.

The Breakout Space connected to a traditional learning space is one example of S-Space that allows educators the opportunity to provide a variety of student grouping sizes. In a 2018 study by Timothy Byers and a group from Melbourne University, a community of connected traditional and breakout spaces was named the Innovative Learning Environment (ILE). The ILE spaces were connected, in some areas, with glass walls, and some were separated from other spaces by opaque walls. The purpose of the study was to understand how teachers and students transitioned from the traditional physical learning environment to the newer flexible physical learning environments. Byers used the linking pedagogy, technology, and space (LPTS) observational metric via a single-subject research design. LPTS includes five domains: pedagogy, learning experiences, communities of learning, student use of technology, and teacher use of technology.

All five domains were impacted by using the ILE. Teacher didactic pedagogies observed in traditional physical learning environments declined in the ILE, while student feedback and engagement increased. Student learning experiences shifted from receiving content to engaging in appraisal and refinement of teacher-provided information. Observations also revealed that the teachers changed their practices to facilitate greater differentiation of activities. The most interesting aspect of this research was that teacher mobility around the room reduced student distractions and increased student engagement. The community of learning domain revealed that students gravitated away from whole classes and individual arrangements toward mixed-size groups. Student and teacher use of technology domains also support a variety of space types as students move among teacher-centered, student-centered, and informal/communal space types within the ILE.

Barriers and challenges were limited but notable. Transparency from space to space via glass walls was distracting at first, but the students overcame this challenge within weeks of using the ILE. Open spaces were intimidating to some students yet enabling to others. Traditionally taught subjects and standardized testing were difficult to provide in the ILE, providing strong support for variety of space types.

Mei-Yung Leung and Ivan Fung (2005) identified decoration and space management as the two most prominent physical features of the S-Space by. Decoration can be defined as the use of space, finish material color, walls, ceiling and floors, and flexible and comfortable furniture. Space management can be defined in two ways: more space and better utilization of the existing space. The latter, a more effective method, can be achieved by using action zones or a variety of teaching/learning spaces created by the configuration of furniture and variety of physical spaces appropriate to the pedagogy.

Leung and Fung (2005) identified two action zone types: chalk and talk, and multimedia. Chalk and talk is the traditional lecture-style learning environment configuration, and multimedia is participatory, interactive, and flexible. When placed in the appropriate action zone, students had an 80% information retention rate. Findings determined that appropriate space management improved students' coordination, attention, classroom preference, and goal achievement. Personalized configurations allowed multiple student ABIs to flourish.

Creative Space or C-Space

C-Spaces encourage creativity. Unlike F-Space, C-Space is designed for exploration and reconfiguration, using movable or flexible partitions, furniture and technology, variations of patterns and textures, and writable surfaces. C-Space encourages critical-thinking and problem-solving skills. These academic spaces are student-centered, where the educator acts as a facilitator in lieu of acting as an instructor. In the workplace, these spaces are for collaboration and the exchange of ideas. C-Spaces include think-tank space, project areas, and medium-to-small group meeting places.

In a 2016 study, Irene White and Francesca Lorenzi (2016) uncovered three C-Space themes (a) C-Space is multidimensional, (b) C-Space has three characterizations, and (c) challenges face the implementation of C-Space into formal physical learning environments.

The first theme identified three dimensions of creativity: physical, social-emotional, and critical. Physical can be defined as physical space; social-emotional can be defined as a safe and supportive environment, valuing student voices; and critical can be defined as encouraging self-motivation and experimentation with ideas. The creative-space physical learning environment was characterized in the second theme by the findings in three ways: open and light, stimulating and cozy, and unexpected and dynamic.

Open and light was defined as minimal physical barriers. Strategically located curtains instead of doors, flexible furniture, and relaxed colors and textures were used to decrease physical and perceived barriers, creating a sense of openness and variety.

Flexible furniture is defined as mobile desk surfaces, chairs, and storage in a variety of types that can be easily reconfigured into multiple orientations. Multiple orientations include face-to-face seating, small group seating, large group seating, and U-shaped or circular configurations. Decentralized technology is defined as individual laptops, tablets, and multiple computer screens for small group use for students and for mobile access to technology by the instructor.

White and Lorenzi (2016) explained that the greatest challenge that faces C-Space implementation within formal physical learning environments is that providing creative pedagogy is in direct conflict with a performance-driven culture that dominates formal education.

When Melissa Rands and Ann Gansemer-Topf (2017) set out to better understand how C-Space impacted student learning, three overarching themes emerged: (a) learning space design encourages a community of learners, (b) learning space design helps students achieve their optimal level of performance, and (c) learning space design encourages students to learn holistically. First, movement, interaction, and removing the student-instructor barrier were the most substantial results of the active learning classroom/space (ALC) in creating a community of learners. The students felt valued as learning process co-constructors. Faculty reflected that movable furniture allowed students to hear each other more effectively. Second, an optimal level of student performance was achieved when students could monitor their own performance using multiple mobile whiteboards, video displays, and writable desktop surfaces. Technology was used in aiding performance when students provided answers using the word cloud on video displays. Portable whiteboards allowed students peer-to-peer interactions when demonstrating work processes. Last, students were encouraged to learn holistically by using both their mind and body to participate in active learning. Engaged active learning stimulated the students' senses.

Most notably, it was discovered the "unexpected" was significant when a student suggested there was always something new to discover every time they walked into the C-Space. The power was in the unexpectedly encouraged students, as co-creators of their physical learning environment, to envision opportunities that stimulated collaboration and interactivity within the group. This holistic learning approach created a sense of community or sense-of-place, consciously and unconsciously, using multiple bodily senses, and allowed the students to retain more information.

With the connectedness of all three space types within the vicinity of each other, you can provide the most equitable environment to address multiple student learning preferences through a greater breadth of individual sense-of-place. Sense-of-place can be created using variations with many configurations of space types to achieve success specific to your PreK–12 district or organization's vision and goals.

Chapter Summary

1. Strong sense-of-place is at the core of every successful PreK–12 District or organization.
2. Sense-of-place is experienced through all five senses and is impacted by activities, meanings, individual features, and physical features.
3. (E x 3) + PE = SOP can be used to measure sense-of-place in any PreK–12 District or organization.
4. Physical features—decentralized technology, flexible furniture, and most importantly the appropriate use of both in a variety of space sizes and types—positively impact student learning.

5

Equity and Inclusion: It's Time for a New Type of Leader to Emerge

Equitable and inclusive learning environments are just as much about addressing individual learning preferences, ABI, as they are about race and gender.

Students have fewer disciplinary issues, less absenteeism, and greater levels of participation and engagement in a student-centered model supported by flexible physical learning environments. Flexible physical learning environments are less restrictive to distractible students and students with disabilities because of the students' ability to break off into smaller groupings in smaller adjacent spaces. Smaller student grouping areas adjacent to larger grouping areas more effectively support special education students than traditional physical learning environments. In terms of gender inclusivity, Landau and Meirovich (2011) provided strong evidence that female students speak more briefly than male students, and they participate less than male students when the learning environment is not perceived to be supportive and safe.

If you go back to Chapter 3, you would find that Meece would agree with this statement. The traditional classroom lacks physical space variety, preventing engagement and equity for individual student learning preferences. Addressing a variety of student learning preferences can potentially create learning environments that stimulate students' senses (Othman & Amiruddin, 2010). Stimulating a variety of individual student learning preferences and students' senses through activities, meanings, individual features, and physical features is the basis of the sense-of-place model.

The National Association of Independent Schools (2017) surveyed more than 10,500 high school students. The study determined that engaged students are more creative and have a higher retention rate than disengaged students: "Engaged students are less likely to drop out and are more satisfied with their coursework" (p. 11). The negative effects on underserved students were decreased by student engagement. Engagement and a sense of belonging, or a sense-of-place, was therefore an important factor for increased emotional, gender, and minority-student equity. From Chapter 4 we understand that engagement is negatively impacted by the traditional physical learning environment in many ways, seating being one of them.

Location, Location, Location

Elisa Park and Bo Keum Choi's (2014) study is one of the most rigorous empirical bodies of research on the negative impact traditional learning environments have on student experience.

The first traditional learning environment survey determined that student experience was impacted by seating location. Four seating zones were created: golden zone, seats located in the front four rows, center two columns; shadow zone, seats in the back of the room, rows 9 and 10 across all six columns; semi-golden zone, the two rows and columns behind and to either side of golden zone seating; and other zone, all other seats in the room. The golden zone, seating preferred by approximately 75% of students, was defined by students in three ways: (a) golden opportunity for eye contact and teacher interaction, (b) best environment for maintaining concentration and motivation; and (c) best view of the whiteboard at the front of the room without distraction from others in the room. Conversely, the shadow zone, seating disliked by approximately 84% of students, was defined in four ways: (a) remote distance from whiteboard, (b) lack of eye contact with instructor, (c) obstruction of views, and (d) distraction from neighboring students.

The most important finding was that the strongest traditional learners got stronger in the traditional learning environment, often at the expense of less confident students. While less confident students desired golden zone seating, they were forced to sit in less desirable seats if they did not arrive early. Conversely, the flexible learning environment created equity for all students regarding interaction, participation, sharing, creating, and learning attitudes.

If there has ever been a metaphor for the established hierarchy that exists in a traditional physical learning environment, it is the static arrangement of seating within a singular box. These inequities and exclusivities quickly dissolve within the variety and connectedness of physical features that flexible physical learning environments engender.

Workplace Exemplar

Unlike schools, employers are creating equity in the workplace by offering a variety of activities and space types that work together (Schittich, 2011). These spaces are engaging and are created out of cognizance of employee needs for a sense-of-place. Employers have done this by decreasing cellular or office spaces and increasing communal spaces for collaborative tasks. Cellular or office space design was popular up until the 1980s. This cost-effective design maximizes building square footage by double loading a corridor with individually functioning rooms. Flexibility for multipurpose space use is limited.

Flexible workplace design provides a variety of space use types. This design meets the needs of business and cultural models that require a high level of collaboration and engagement (Schittich, 2011). Although flexible workplace design is less cost effective than cellular office design, it is required to support an increased sense-of-place among space users.

When We Focus on ABI, Everyone Wins

Equity and inclusion are not exclusive to race and gender only. Equity and inclusion will be more holistically achieved when we provide educational environments that address each student's ABI. Go back to Chapter 3 for a moment. Refresh your Abilities, Background, and Interests knowledge. ABI is the lens we should be using to approach equity and inclusion. Race and gender fit within ABI, not vice versa. When we approach individuals' needs instead of placing students in systemic boxes, via race or gender labels, we get to the root cause of what lights a fire under a child, what approach they will respond to most favorably, and what will get them engaged. Race or gender is what they are; ABI is who they are, how they provide the most value to themselves—dignity, their family, and the community at large, and why they ultimately exist.

BCE vs. CE = "Before the COVID-19" Era vs. "COVID-19" Era

The COVID-19 pandemic has opened our eyes to the inequitable access to educational opportunities for all learners. We are now more aware that the inequity has existed for a long time. Let's call this, BCE, "Before the COVID-19 Era," a play on the nondenominational reference to, "Before the Common Era." Within the Christian community, BC is used.

We now know how much we had taken for granted; the privileges that we enjoyed at the expense of others. Are we going to use this opportunity to make meaningful change? Are we going to provide the opportunities to empower our children so they may create their own CE, "Common Era" or for the sake of this conversation, the, "COVID-19 Era" that will influence all future events? We may not experience this level of global self-awareness again. Remember 9-11? Right and Left holding hands for the common interest of overcoming a singular threat against Democracy. Remember BLM? We do now, but where will that movement be a year from now? There is urgency for us to act now before our self-awareness is inevitably diluted in cyclical fashion by the everyday cadence of life.

6

If It's So Important, Why Are We Not Evolving?

According to the U.S. Department of Education's "Condition of America's Public School Facilities: 2012–13" report (Alexander et al., 2014), school districts in the United States spent $14 billion on construction projects. According to the report, "53% of public schools needed modernization to be considered in good overall condition" Despite the need and the means to modernize the national school system, school environment design has not evolved in pace with workplace environment design. PreK–12 learning environment design continues to follow the traditional learning environment model. In addition, learning environment design innovation has seen limited support from state and national governments in the United States (Washor & Mojkowski, 2003).

According to a 2015 study by the Education Week Research Center, PreK–12 schools in the United States have not made the financial commitment to social and creative pedagogies that support social and emotional learning. As of 2015, only 34% of educators had implemented these pedagogies, yet approximately 99% of educators interviewed believed in the perceived benefits of social and emotional learning supported by flexible physical learning environments (Education Week Research Center, 2015).

The desire to create student sense-of-place is present, yet many PreK–12 stakeholders are reluctant to make the change and implement flexible physical learning environments in their school districts (Kennedy, 2015). There are many reasons for this reluctance. The first and most critical: meaningful change, in all its forms, is painful. The growth process is operationally complex and physically disruptive. District leadership must be internally cohesive and have a strong relationship with the community they serve. Change management expertise is essential to move a PreK–12 organizational culture beyond the following challenges:

1. Risk-averse nature of PreK–12 administrators. In recent years, the role of district leadership has become more a balancing act of stakeholders, in

survival mode, than exploring innovative methods for transcending the status quo. You can't ask people to get on the bus if others keep letting the air out of the tires.

2. Administrators' fear of creating inequity between schools within a district when limited resources narrow the number of schools scheduled for a physical learning environment design change. Annual budgets are always tight, and district administrators are being asked to provide increased services with less funding every year. Creating districtwide equity takes the use of creative funding sources over many years, in most cases. A trajectory for change is just that, and long-range planning is most often required.

3. PTSD of trends that come and go. The failure of the open classroom model (non-traditional classroom) haunts us to this day. We now know why non-traditional classrooms failed and can use these lessons learned by providing flexible learning environments that are balanced, allowing opportunities supportive of educators eager to address multiple student ABIs.

4. Educator allegiance to the traditional classroom model and educator territoriality. *Educator Allegiance*–Most of us have been educated in a traditional learning environment. Most of our educators have been educated in a traditional learning environment, and most of our PreK–12 administrators are former teachers educated in a traditional learning environment. *Educator*

Territoriality–A fish will only grow as large as its bowl will allow. An educator can only grow if the learning environment is adaptable to flexible pedagogies and space. More importantly, an educator will return to traditional methods if not given appropriate Professional Development (PD) to support new methods.

PD must happen using both regularly scheduled organized methods and organic methods. *Organized PD* is typically ineffective—first, because it happens only once or twice a year, and second, like a traditional teaching method is provided as a one-size-fits-all solution for large groups of educators. PD becomes a formality and enthusiasm fades when not reinforced frequently. *Organic PD* happens when educators are provided with the opportunity to collaborate. This can only happen in a flexible learning environment, via teacher-to-student and teacher-to-teacher mentoring. Organic PD finds even greater promise when educators are given flexible learning environments supporting teacher-to-teacher mentoring that allows them the space to model the way for student-occupied spaces.

Educator PD Space

A 2014 case study was unique in its provision of flexible learning environments for educators with the aim of progressing toward a more personalized, student-centered model. The physical features of the Teaching Grid, a flexible physical learning environment for educators, were studied to determine future use of the same physical features for student learning environments. The Teaching

Grid was a mock space for PD to simulate the future of student-occupied flexible physical learning environments. The Teaching Grid provided a chance for the educators to work in a flexible and customizable physical space that provided a variety of peer-to-peer collaborative and technology-rich environment options (King et al., 2014).

The physical features of the Teaching Grid included a variety of mobile furniture types: round tables, square tables, and rectangular tables, with the capacity to seat two, four, six, or eight in different configurations. Individual couch seating and sectional seating were also provided. Technology was mobile. The most important physical features that link the Teaching Grid to Jankowska and Atlay's F-Space, S-Space, and C-Space were provided by flexible glass panels and curtains on tracks. Movable glass panel partitions and translucent curtains provided space types of multiple sizes and shapes for a variety of sizes of group activities, with visibility to other complementing spaces.

Ultimately, the study findings of the Teaching Grid reinforced flexibility in allowing educators a variety of pedagogies that were not feasible in traditional teaching/learning environments. The option to use a variety of pedagogies allowed educators the opportunity to address an array of student learning preferences/ABIs, creating more holistic organizational sense-of-place.

Educator PD space is one example of a centralized method to get the ball rolling on your trajectory for an eventual decentralized mentoring model. Organic mentoring, both teacher-to-student and teacher-to-teacher, embraced by teacher champions, supported by flexible teaching and learning environments, is essential to creating the most effective student-centered learning model.

7

A Recipe for Success: How You Can Be a Champion for Change

School district- and school-level leaders must provide a districtwide mission of inclusivity grounded in sense-of-place addressing multiple student learning preferences, ABIs. As teachers provide a safe environment for student expression, PreK–12 leadership must provide teachers with permission, support, and advocacy for innovation. Reciprocally, teachers must take advantage of district leadership opportunities by becoming champions for change.

By using student-centered learning approaches in flexible physical learning environments that do a better a job of reaching more students, teachers can be change agents for greater inclusivity. Boards of education need to act on administrator recommendations for physical space that promotes equitable opportunities for greater engagement. State policy makers need to welcome design solutions from architects that safely break down barriers preventing collaboration by increasing a variety of space sizes and types adjacent to each other that promote student grouping opportunities. Community members must demand more sustainable and equitable environments for their children.

District and School Administrators

PreK–12 school district and school leaders must provide more sustainable education for their students. First, district and school leaders must provide a district-wide mission of inclusivity grounded in sense-of-place to address multiple student learning preferences.

Second, district and school leaders must provide permission, support, and protection for their teachers. Initially, they can do this by giving permission to the teachers to be innovative and creative in their teaching methods. Teachers should be encouraged to ask the "what if" questions. Then, leaders have to encourage and support teacher initiatives for change, and leaders need to provide support to teachers as they pilot initiatives through to completion. Providing permission for and support of experimentation with teacher-led flexible learning space initiatives allows teachers to do a better job at reaching more students through their unique learning preferences.

Lastly, district and building leaders must walk the talk. Leaders need to show their support for flexible physical learning environments. District and school leaders must provide data that support and communicate the benefits of flexible physical learning environments by working closely with experts in the field.

District leadership must facilitate meetings and tours of schools and classrooms in other districts that have similar missions and flexible physical learning environment renovation projects. *Seeing is believing.* District and school leaders must provide teachers with the opportunity to apply lessons learned from these tours using student-centered teaching methods to create prototypes of flexible physical learning environments in their own schools.

Teachers

Teachers are the "boots on the ground" in the fight for meaningful and equitable change. If they are so lucky to have leadership that is ready to provide permission, support, and advocacy of a mission for sustainable inclusivity, they must take advantage of this opportunity. Teachers can take advantage of this opportunity by being open to new ideas, being proactive, and trusting the process that their leaders have laid in front of them. Teachers should volunteer to become champions for change and tour exemplar schools to get firsthand knowledge.

Teachers must explore and implement student-centered learning and teaching methods that reach more students. Student-centered learning and teaching methods shift the focus of instruction away from the instructor and onto the student. The educator acts as a facilitator, encouraging student autonomy and independent problem solving. Further, teachers must be prepared to embrace the learning curve that flexible learning environments require. New physical features include interconnected rooms of varying size and shape, mobile furniture and technology; and architectural elements such as movable partitions, doors, and finishes. Teachers can embrace these decentralizing features that allow student and teacher engagement.

Policy Makers

State policy makers and boards of education play a key role by acting as advocates for the implementation of flexible physical learning environments. They have the power to create new opportunities by developing policies of architectural design that encourage greater inclusivity supported by flexible physical learning environments. Flexible physical learning environments promote emotional intelligence skills that are increasingly required by employers today. Therefore, policy makers hold the key to workforce development, as well. The perceived change to flexible physical learning environments can be a challenge, as traditional physical learning environments have been a staple of our educational identity for so long.

Policy makers at state education departments can either welcome or prevent flexible physical learning environment architectural design elements based on their interpretations of the building codes they use and enforce with PreK–12 education facilities. In unique circumstances, state planning and design standards create a barrier to sense-of-place physical features that allow inclusivity via collaboration of adjacent spaces. How do we change that?

First, state policy makers must regularly update their standards, regulations, and building codes to address the evolving nature of educational environments that support the emotional intelligence skills that students need, educators crave, and employers now require.

Second, state policy makers do not need to start from scratch. They can look to exemplar state education departments and facilities planning departments for flexible physical learning environment guidance and best practices.

School district boards of education represent the voice of district community members. First, boards of education must work closely with district leadership and experts in the field to act in the best interest of all students. This means ensuring environments that allow for inclusivity of all student learning preferences. Second, boards of education must act on leadership recommendations when they are provided with credible data that support flexible physical learning environments.

Community Members

Parents, family members, mentors, and professionals within the community, you are the advocates for young students, the future of your community. Now that you have a better understanding how the learning environment impacts your children's learning, it's time to advocate for pedagogy and space that meet the needs of their sense-of-place. Now is also the time to advocate for those children that do not have advocates by creating learning environments that welcome all children and their ABIs.

Call to Action

Flexible learning environments provide too many opportunities for improving the current state of education to continue to be ignored. The traditional physical learning environment is not an effective model for educating today's and tomorrow's students. Flexible learning environments remove the obstacles to student inclusivity and benefit all stakeholders.

This book may assist districts and educational organizations that are having trouble shifting their educational paradigm. This book may also serve as an important genesis for educators and architects with convincing evidence that flexible physical learning environments do more to help our children find their sense-of-place. Sense-of-place transcends existing traditional learning environments and educates our future leaders as lifelong learners.

Providing flexible physical learning environments is the obligation of all to foster change and more effectively serve all students and families.

Are you ready to take on the challenge and become a Flexible Physical Learning Environment Champion for Change?

About the Author

Dr. Joseph C. Kosiorek is a forward-thinking planner, designer, and leader who has spent his career developing a unique understanding of PreK–12 learning environments. Dr. Kosiorek is at the forefront of the PreK–12 educational design renaissance, guiding districts that have an interest in creating equitable and inclusive environments that foster the potential of students' learning preferences and progressive teaching methods that prepare students for success. His clients trust his guidance throughout the entire development process, from education planning to districtwide master planning, for garnering community involvement and support, maximizing state funding, providing educator space use professional development, and implementing capital improvement projects. Dr. Kosiorek also provides a unique focus on corporate strategic planning, and business development.

Dr. Kosiorek applies his dedication and understanding of PreK–12 learning environments to assist his clients with safety plans for reopening schools during the COVID-19 crisis. He is working with districts to find solutions that not only keep the students and staff safe but will also provide equitable learning opportunities for the future.

As an architect, Dr. Kosiorek has over 20 years of regional, full-service, programming, pre-referendum, design, management, and construction administration experience. He has worked on a variety of school and commercial facilities, with work encompassing new building design, building renovations and additions, and existing building condition surveys.

References

Adedokun, O. A., Henke, J. N., Parker, L. C., & Burgess, W. D. (2017). Student perceptions of a 21st century learning space. *Journal of Learning Spaces, 6*(1), 1–13.

Ahlfeldt, S., Mehta, S., & Sellnow, T. (2005). Measurement and analysis of student engagement in university classes where varying levels of PBL methods of instruction are in use. *Higher Education Research & Development, 24*(1), 5–20.

Alexander, D., Lewis, L., & Ralph, J. (2014, March). *Condition of America's public school facilities: 2012–13: First look.* NCES, IES, U.S. Department of Education. https://nces.ed.gov/pubs2014/2014022.pdf

Baker, L. (2012, January). *A history of school design and its indoor environmental standards, 1900 to today.*

National Clearinghouse for Educational Facilities. http://www.ncef.org/pubs/greenschoolshistory.pdf

Barker, R. G. (1968). *Ecological psychology: Concepts and methods for studying the environment of human behavior.* Stanford University Press.

Bekerman, Z., Burbules, N. C., & Silberman-Keller, D. (2006). *Learning in places: The informal education reader.* Peter Lang.

Byers, T., Imms, W., & Hartnell-Young, E. (2018). Evaluating teacher and student spatial transition from a traditional classroom to an innovative learning environment. *Studies in Educational Evaluation, 58,* 156–166.

Education Week Research Center. (2015). *Social and emotional learning: Perspectives from America's schools.* http://www.edweek.org/media/ewrc_selreport_june2015.pdf

Falahat, M. S. (2006). The sense of place and its factors. *Honar-ha-ye-Ziba, 26,* 57–66. https://www.researchgate.net/figure/The-model-of-important-factors-forming-sense-of-place-Falahat-2006_fig2_283170578

Falahat, M. S., Kamali, L., & Shahidi, S. (2017). The role of the "sense of place" concept in improving architectural conservation quality. *Bagh-e Nazar,*

14(46), 17–26. https://www.researchgate.net/publication/320058736_The_Role_of_the_Sense_of_Place_Concept_in_Improving_Architectural_Conservation_Quality

Gallup, Inc. (2016). *Gallup student poll engaged today – Ready for tomorrow: U.S. overall: 2015 score card.* https://kidsathope.org/wp-content/uploads/2015/05/2015-Gallup-Student-Poll-Overall-Report.pdf

Georgiou, D., Carspecken, P. F., & Willems, E. P. (1996). An expansion of Roger Barker's behavior setting survey for an ethno-ecological approach to person–environment interactions. *Journal of Environmental Psychology, 16*(4), 319–333.

Ginsburg, K. R. (2011). *Building resilience in children and teens: Giving kids roots and wings.* American Academy of Pediatrics.

Gladwell, M. (2013). *Outliers: The story of success.* Back Bay Books.

Jalili, T., & Azar, A. (2016). Phenomenology of sense of place and its constituents in children educational environments. *International Journal of Humanities and Cultural Studies, 3*(2), 862–870.

Jankowska, M., & Atlay, M. (2008). Use of creative space in enhancing students' engagement. *Innovations in*

Education and Teaching International, 45(3), 271–279. doi:10.1080/14703290802176162

Jerald, C. D. (2009). *Defining a 21st century education.* The Center for Public Education. http://citeseerx.ist.psu.edu/viewdoc/download?doi=10.1.1.460.8011&rep=rep1&type=pdf

Kennedy, M. (2015). The future is now. *American School & University, 87*(8), 13.

King, E., Joy, M., Foss, J., Sinclair, J., & Sitthiworachart, J. (2014). Exploring the impact of a flexible, technology-enhanced teaching space on pedagogy. *Innovations in Education and Teaching International, 52*(5), 1–14.

Landau, J., & Meirovich, G. (2011). Development of students' emotional intelligence: Participative classroom environments in higher education. *Academy of Educational Leadership Journal, 15*(3), 89–104.

Lengen, C., & Kistemann, T. (2012). Sense of place and place identity: Review of neuroscientific evidence. *Health and Place, 18*(5), 1162–1171.

Leung, M., & Fung, I. (2005). Enhancement of classroom facilities of primary schools and its impact on learning behaviors of students. *Facilities, 23*(13/14), 585–594. https://doi.org/10.1108/02632770510627561

Lin, C., & Lockwood, M. (2014). Assessing sense of place in natural settings: A mixed-method approach. *Journal of Environmental Planning and Management, 57*(10), 1441–1464.

Loveless, T. (2015, March). *The 2015 Brown Center report on American education: How well are American students learning?* Brown Center on Education Policy at Brookings. https://www.brookings.edu/wp-content/uploads/2016/06/2015-Brown-Center-Report_FINAL-3.pdf

Meece, J. (2003). Applying learner-centered principles to middle school education. *Theory Into Practice, 42*(2), 109–116.

Nair, P. (2014, September/October). From "cells and bells" to learning communities: Renovating school facilities for student-centered learning. *Harvard Education Letter, 30*(5). https://www.hepg.org/hel-home/issues/30_5/helarticle/from-cells-and-bells-to-learning-communities

National Association of Independent Schools. (2017). *NAIS report on the 2016 high school survey of student engagement.* Retrieved from https://www.fcis.org/uploaded/Data_Reports/2016-HSSSE_Final_1.pdf

National Center for Education Statistics. (2015). *Program for International Student Assessment (PISA).* https://nces.ed.gov/surveys/pisa/index.asp

National Survey of Student Engagement. (2000). *National Survey of Student Engagement: The college student report: The NSSE 2000 report: National benchmarks of effective educational practice*. https://files.eric.ed.gov/fulltext/ED464569.pdf

National Training Laboratories Institute (2018). *Learning Pyramid, Average Retention Rates Model*. https://www.bing.com/search?q=average%20retention%20rates%20passive%20teaching%20participatory%20&qs=n&form=QBRE&sp=-1&pq=average%20retention%20rates%20passive%20teaching%20participatory%20&sc=0-55&sk=&cvid=25F39E6180A94AD39CDF17D2B2D59B58

Othman, N., & Amiruddin, M. (2010). Different perspectives of learning styles from VARK model. *Procedia - Social and Behavioral Sciences*, *7*, 652–660. https://doi.org/10.1016/j.sbspro.2010.10.088

Park, E., & Choi, B. K. (2014). Transformation of classroom spaces: Traditional versus active learning classroom in colleges. *Higher Education*, *68*(5), 749–771.

Parsons, C. S. (2017). Reforming the environment: The influences of the roundtable classroom design on interactive learning. *Journal of Learning Spaces*, *6*(3), 23–33.

Popov, L., & Chompalov, I. (2012). Crossing over: The interdisciplinary meaning of behavior setting theory. *International Journal of Humanities and Social Science, 2*(19), 18–27.

Proshansky, H. M., Ittelson, W. H., & Rivlin, L. G. (1976). *Environmental psychology: People and their physical settings*. Holt, Rinehart and Winston.

Rands, M. L., & Gansemer-Topf, A. M. (2017). The room itself is active: How classroom design impacts student engagement. *Journal of Learning Spaces, 6*(1), 26–33.

Riener, C., & Willingham, D. (2010). The myth of learning styles. *Change: The Magazine of Higher Learning, 42*(5), 32–35.

Schittich, C. (Ed.). (2011). *In DETAIL: Work environments: Spatial concepts, usage strategies, communications*. Redaktion DETAIL.

Scott, M. (2005). A powerful theory and a paradox: Ecological psychologists after Barker. *Environment and Behavior, 37*(3), 295–329.

Uzzaman, M., & Karim, A. (2018). Family and school environment in relation to adolescents emotional intelligence and future aspiration. *Indian Journal of Positive Psychology, 9*(3), 413–422.

Vali, A. P., & Nasekhiyan, S. (2014). The concept and sense of place in architecture from phenomenological approach. *Indian Journal of Fundamental and Applied Life Sciences, 4*(S4), 3746–3753. http://www.cibtech.org/sp.ed/jls/2014/04/JLS-446-S4-448-AMIRHOOSEIN-CONCEPT.pdf

Washor, E., & Mojkowski, C. G. (2003). *Translating innovative pedagogical designs into school facilities designs* (Doctoral dissertation). Retrieved from ProQuest Dissertations. (3106417)

White, I., & Lorenzi, F. (2016). The development of a model of creative space and its potential for transfer from non-formal to formal education. *International Review of Education, 62*(6), 771–790.

www.ingramcontent.com/pod-product-compliance
Lightning Source LLC
Chambersburg PA
CBHW072017290426
44109CB00018B/2269